Transitions

TRANSITIONS

Prayers and

Declarations for a

Changing Life

JULIA
CAMERON

PAN BOOKS

First published in the United States of America in 1999
by Jeremy P. Tarcher / Putnam, a member of Penguin Putnam Inc.

First published in Great Britain 2000 by Pan Books
an imprint of Macmillan Publishers Ltd
25 Eccleston Place, London SW1W 9NF
Basingstoke and Oxford
Associated companies throughout the world
www.macmillan.co.uk

ISBN 0 330 39189 5

3 5 7 9 8 6 4 2

A CIP catalogue record for this book is available from
the British Library.

Book design by Claire Vaccaro

Printed and bound in Great Britain by
Mackays of Chatham plc, Chatham, Kent

In loving memoriam

Shari Lewis

I wish to acknowledge two gentlemen
whose artfulness shaped this book:

TIM WHEATER, *composer*
JEREMY TARCHER, *editor*

And two gentlewomen:

EMMA LIVELY, *musician*
DORI VINELLA, *muse*

INTRODUCTION

The window of my writing room looks north to Taos Mountain. For me, that mountain is my great teacher. At one moment it looms dark purple against the horizon. Moments later, it is lit by gold. Its folds are crimson and bronze, a transition that happened while I was writing, my attention absorbed by the page.

"Everything changes, is always changing," the mountain reminds me. And yet, it reminds me, too, "There is a bedrock, a level of spiritual reality, that remains always the same."

This book concerns change: the difficulty of change, the possibility of change. It also, at ground level, concerns the acceptance of change. So often we try to live through our changes without experiencing them. When life is difficult, we tune out, focused on the future. "I will be happy," we say, "when this happens" or "when that happens." Or else we say, "I will be happy when this is over." Or, "When that begins."

Focused on life as we yearn for it, we neglect to live the life that we have. "This shouldn't be happening," we tell ourselves in difficult seasons. Meaning, "Once this is over, I'll get on with my life."

Craving the comfort of desired events and outcomes, we ignore the uncomfortable but exhilarating gifts of living life as a continually unfolding process in which all moments are valuable. Absorbed in our "inner movie," we miss the many minute transformations that enrich and ennoble our lives.

In meditation, whether it is three pages of longhand morning writing or twenty minutes of sitting observing our breath, we learn to see the flow of thoughts and perceptions which accompany our lives like a soundtrack. We learn to note and notice our rapidly shifting moods to see that we are the someone who stands somehow apart from those moods, experiencing them like clouds on the face of the mountain. This is the gift of detachment. The prayers in these pages aim at conveying such a gift.

It is usually the emotional burden of a difficult circumstance that causes us to move through it numbly, cut off from our spiritual resources. A sudden illness, the death of a spouse, the unexpected loss of a treasured job, a cherished friend's moving away—any of these may be sufficient to disconnect us from our ongoing sense of the fruitfulness and purpose of life.

"What does it all mean, anyhow?" we may conclude at such moments. Our shadowed hearts are cut off from the sunlight of the spirit. When we enter such a darkened place it is hard to believe that God, or goodness, can accompany us there.

This book is intended as a conscious companion for difficult times. The prayers directly address many of the difficult transitions that we as humans undergo. This book, however, is intended as something more than a companion. It is also planned as a model for you to work from. The quotes are carefully selected and provocative. I have written my prayers inspired by them and you can as well. The writing of positive, affirmative prayers is a deeply healing spiritual antidote to the pain of anguished moments. Let me give you an example.

The poet Kabir writes, "Wherever you are is the entry point," and that is how to work with writing a prayer. You might write like this:

"WHEREVER YOU ARE IS THE ENTRY POINT"

℘ "I stand at the doorway. I am entering the door to my new life. That life is lit by friendship, graced by music, freshly painted because color speaks to my heart . . ."

Taking the same quote, you might equally well write like this:

& "I pause as I enter the gate of a new relationship. I take stock of who I am and what I am as myself alone. I appreciate my humor and autonomy, my intellectual curiosity and my creative daring. These I resolve to keep with me. I will retain and cherish my 'I' within our 'We.'"

Equally, you might write:

& "I am at the threshold of a new business life. I am strong and creative as I step toward my new opportunity. The very gifts that have served me in the past, serve me now. I walk ahead with confidence and conviction in my own competence."

Use this book as a companion in challenging times and as a catalyst to write prayers of your own. It is my experience in many years as an artist and teacher that writing "rights" things. As we move our hand across the canvas of our lives, we paint more vividly the brush-strokes of our experience. Writing is transformative, alchemical, empowering and enlightening.

Our transitions become more consciously wrought. As we choose to enter into and cooperate with a difficult passage, we light that passage with the lamp of our personal compassion. By choosing not to abandon ourselves during trying times, we discover the constancy of the Universe loving through us despite all harrowing appearances. When we write the word "I" and claim our experience, we enter the "eye" of the storm, allowing ourselves a steadiness and spiritual constancy even in the midst of strife. It is my hope that this book will be for you both a harbor and a boat.

However confused
the scene of our life appears,
however torn we may be
who now do face that scene,
it can be faced,
and we can go on to be whole.

MURIEL RUKEYSER

Spirit understands adversity as opportunity. Spirit is able to work for the good in all things. As I encounter difficult transitions in which I doubt the good which is unfolding, I remind myself there is a higher plan in motion with which I can consciously cooperate. As I face my resistance to change, as I choose to align myself with events as they are unfolding, I find in my acceptance a sense of tranquility, a promise of safety. Change embraces me as I myself embrace change.

  ❦ Today, I surrender my resistance to my hidden yet greater good. I cast my faith forward as a light on my path. I choose to believe in the good which comes toward me. I release my fear.

Every moment
of one's existence
one is growing into more
or retreating into less.
One is always living
a little more
or dying a little bit.

NORMAN MAILER

ᕤ

All change can be expansive in potential. The choice is ours. As I open my heart to accept change, my heart softens and grows larger. Every experience carries the seed of transformation. Every event can bring blossoming and wealth. My personal will can resist change or embrace it. The choice is mine and determines the life I will have.

ᕤ Today, I choose to embrace change. I open my heart to its hidden but abundant blessings.

The natural world teaches us the power of change. As seasons shift, I see the purpose and beauty of life's cyclicality. I see the promise of spring, the ripening of summer, the bounty of harvest and the mysterious containment of winter. All seasons work for the good. So it is, too, with the changing cycles of my life. As I surrender to the wisdom of a higher plan, I discover in all circumstances the opportunity for growth and expansion. There is no season in my life that is without worth. There is no season in my life that does not unfold my highest good. Challenged by difficult times, I consciously choose to affirm the goodness of life's timing.

❧ Today, I commit myself to actively seeking the benefit hidden in adversity, the wisdom inherent in all timing.

Wisdom lies
neither in fixity
nor in change,
but in the dialectic
between the two.

OCTAVIO PAZ

☙

Curiosity is the right companion of change. It is an attitude that we must elect to hold. As I embrace an attitude of curiosity and wonder, change brings me growth and renewal. It is the key of curiosity which opens the gate to my greater unfolding. As I open my mind and heart, subtle blessings are revealed to me. Life gains new and unexpected graces, colors, textures and benefits. Curiosity empowers me to explore new dimensions. Curiosity brings me optimism and hope during difficult times.

Today, I embrace my curious nature. I allow curiosity to lead me forward in positive ways through adversity and hardship. My curiosity seeks and discovers buried gifts in all experience.

Today the world changes
so quickly
that in growing up
we take leave
not just of youth
but of the world
we were young in . . .
Fear and resentment
of what is new
is really a lament
for the memories of our childhood.

SIR PETER MEDAWAR

Resistance solidifies grief. We can allow our griefs to dissolve through releasing them to the healing rain of tears. As we weep with loss, our spiritual landscape is made anew. All change carries gain as well as loss. As I release situations which have troubled me, I release, too, my identity as troubled. This shift brings with it intense emotion. Grief is the natural and healing companion of loss. Embraced and surrendered to, grief creates transformation.

☙ Today, I do not deny my feelings of loss. I allow myself to move through them to new growth.

No one's death comes to pass
without making some impression,
and those close to the deceased
inherit part of the liberated soul
and become richer in their humaneness.

HERMANN BROCH

All of life is interconnected and ongoing. There is no death to the spirit of those I love. As I mourn the physical passing of my beloveds, I open to meet them anew in an ongoing spiritual connection. Subtle but resilient, our relationship goes forward. As I open my heart to continued connection, I encounter the spark of intuition, the lamp of guidance which signals the shared ongoing path. Those who leave me do so only in body. The physical vehicle falls away but the beloved spirit continues to live and even to prosper. Ours is a journey of shared hearts. Death is a passageway, not an ending. As I open my heart to continued connection, my beloveds are carried forward by my love.

🖎 Today, I am brave enough to open to continued connection. I am alert to small signs and signals which speak to me of my beloveds' ongoing presence.

The Lord continually creates,
sustains,
and absorbs all.
He performs all tasks.

SWAMI MUKTANANDA

◌

S pirit is all-pervasive. Absolutely nothing exists beyond its healing reach. As I move forward through difficult change, Spirit goes before me, preparing a path for me to follow. In Spirit's hands, all change is beneficial. All change works toward the good. There is no problem too small or too large for Spirit to heal and transform. Every detail of my life is relevant to Spirit. There is nothing that I face that I must face alone. In all times of difficulty and discomfort, I turn to Spirit for aid and sustenance. Spirit nurtures me in all circumstances, supports me at every turn.

Today, I open my heart to accept the help which I am given in all things, both large and small. Today I acknowledge and salute the God force acting in all my affairs.

Friendship is one of the most
tangible things
in a world which offers
fewer and fewer supports.

KENNETH BRANAGH

☙

My human loves are cherished companions. I treasure the times we spend together. I salute the importance of our connection, yet I recognize that there are times of appropriate distance. Such transits require an adjustment in attitude. Our hearts must expand rather than contract from loss. In times of separation, I affirm that our connection remains intact through Spirit. Spirit leads our loving hearts and Spirit knows no distance or separation. In Spirit, all things are near, all times are one eternal moment. Taking my lesson from this great teaching, I celebrate connection and continuity in the face of apparent abandonment and loss.

 Today, I acknowledge that all things are one through Spirit. I affirm the presence in the present moment of those who have moved beyond my reach.

Every incident is nourishing,
every circumstance is nourishing,
every word is nourishing,
every sound is nourishing,
because the same love
is in everything and in everyone.

SWAMI CHIDVILASANANDA

Nourishment is spiritual. It is always available to us. The power that we seek is spiritual as well as temporal. In the face of waning health of the body, I affirm a growing health in spirit. Spirit is victorious over illness and even death. Spirit lives on undaunted by physical decline. My spirit is strong and courageous. My spirit is larger than adverse circumstances. I expand into spiritual realms seeking a higher and longer view of current events. As I view the overriding good that works through all and in all, I am able to embrace my destiny and claim the good which it contains.

⚘ Today, I claim my spiritual health. I bless and celebrate perfect life within me. I acknowledge that I am a child of the Divine and that my divinity is untouched by adverse conditions. My spirit is triumphant, nourished by God.

This world is nothing but a school of love;
our relationships with our
husband or wife,
with our children and parents,
with our friends and relatives
are the university in which we are meant
to learn what love and devotion
truly are.

SWAMI MUKTANANDA

All of earth is my home. I am nurtured in every place, in every situation. As I leave behind that which is familiar, I find new places where I also find love. Bearing goodwill I find goodwill. I encounter harmony and openness in those I meet. I am embraced. My spirit finds shelter. In my new home, new friends welcome me, making a valued place for me in their lives. I am not alone. Friendships find me.

Today, I embrace the new. I allow my heart to find joy and connection with new companions. I make my heart the hearth at which I warm my spirit. I am at home in every place.

Divine wisdom underlies all events. No change is without the possibility of benefit. No transition, however harrowing and difficult, fails to bring good. Despite appearances to the contrary, all events unfold according to a higher harmony. I attune myself to this unfolding. I release my doubts, fears and misgivings to a higher hand. By asking Spirit to comfort me, I am cradled in my human frailty yet strengthened in my spiritual connection. I turn to Spirit in all circumstances. I open to the higher good that unfolds through my compliance.

Today, I acknowledge the presence of Spirit in all circumstances. I attune myself to the higher plan that works through me and for me. I expect help and accept it. Divine consciousness is attuned to my needs. I am not unheard.

All the creatures of this cosmos
are sustained by love,
and in the end they merge into
the same cosmic Being.
That is why it is essential to love.

SWAMI MUKTANANDA

In the divine plan I am partnered by nature—the crimson flash of a cardinal on the wing, the Persian's inscrutable gaze, the silken coat of the cocker spaniel curled by my feet—these are animal companions whom I hold dear. My teachers as well as my friends, my animal companions instruct me to live with devotion and harmony, forgiving slights and inattentions, loving with a sweet and attentive heart. Briefer lived than I, my animal companions teach the joy of living fully, in every moment. As they pass from my realm, I thank them for their selfless love, for the many merry moments that we shared. Bearing their memory in my heart, I am a better companion to all of life.

CҀ Today, I salute my animal friends. I celebrate their passage through my life. I allow them to accompany me and also to guide me. I accept their devotion and offer my devoted love in return.

Be a lamp, or a lifeboat, or a ladder.
Help someone's soul heal.
Walk out of your house like a shepherd.

RUMI

ove requires generosity. Love requires daring and expansion. Above all, love requires a dance of differing distances. There is both the pas de deux and the time for solo flight. The dance of love contains both turns. While cherishing our shared time together, I freely release my beloveds to pursue a separate path if that is their destiny. Love connects despite distance. I hold my beloveds tenderly in my heart, trusting that the distance that separates us also brings us together, gifting us with a stronger appreciation of our unique bond. Freedom is a requirement of real love. I honor my beloveds with the gift of freedom.

୧ Today, I open my hand. I release my loved ones to their separate and unique destinies. I cherish them tenderly within my heart while flinging aside the ropes of control that might bind them. I love with an open hand and a resilient heart.

It isn't for the moment
you are struck that you need courage,
but for the long uphill climb
back to sanity
and faith and security.

ANNE MORROW LINDBERGH

⁂

I nurture a faithful heart. When difficulties, sorrows, and trials beset me, I consciously choose faith in the face of despair. Like the mountain climber who reaches the summit a step at a time, I hold an ideal in my heart. Despite the temptation to bitterness, despite the seduction of rage, I choose a path of temperate endurance, grounding my daily life in the small joys yet available to me. Learning from the natural world, I harbor the seeds of hope against the long winter. I count the small stirrings of beauty and delight still present in a barren time. My heart is a seasoned traveler. Moving through hostile and unfamiliar terrain it remains alert to encounter unexpected beauty blossoming despite the odds. In the arms of adversity, I yet find the comfort of tenderness to myself and others. I refuse to harbor a hardened heart. Decisively and deliberately, I expand rather than contract.

⟨ Today, I choose the softening grace of forgiveness. I allow the sunlight of the spirit to reach my shadowed heart.

Kabir says this: just throw away all
thoughts of imaginary things,
and stand firm in that which you are.

KABIR

The human heart craves certainty yet life is
sometimes uncertain. In times of ambiguity,
doubt and apprehension, I claim the certain
safety of my spiritual connection. Reminding myself
that even in the face of difficult change, my grounding
in Spirit remains secure, I find ground on which to
stand. Spirit connects me to all things. It is timeless
and serene. Spirit is the bedrock beneath all experience.
When I am threatened and adrift, I remind myself
Spirit is an inner fortress, constant and secure.

Today, I embrace Spirit as the rock of my existence. Spirit gives my soul an earthly home.

All who joy would win
Must share it—Happiness was born
a twin.

LORD BYRON

ometimes we are less a person than a place for those we love. Our hearts are the hearth sought by the lonely. I offer those I love the steadiness of my companionship when times grow difficult and dark. Recognizing that my familiar presence offers comfort and dignity to those I cherish, I stand my ground, rooted in the love between us. As my beloveds undergo difficult passages, I walk beside them. I offer compassion, humor, honor for their strength. I am a loving witness. I am steadfast, loyal and strong for those I love.

⊂ঌ Today, I celebrate my role as companion to those I love. I offer witness and good cheer. I light the steady lamp of compassionate attention. My heart is a lantern guide for those I love.

When one man dies,
one chapter is not torn out of the book,
but translated into a better language.

JOHN DONNE

The soul is a traveler through the realm of matter. Our bodies are beloved vehicles housing our souls. The soul is eternal and moves on when it is finished here. The death we see as final is just a door. Faced with the death of one I love, I offer my loving witness of their passage. Grounded in the spiritual truth that life endures, I offer comfort and companionship as my beloved faces the great unknown. Rather than surrender to my own feelings of loss and bereavement, I assure my beloved of love's continuity. Our physical parting does not sever our spiritual ties. Love is the affirmation of life in the face of death. Love is life expanding, living on ever after.

☙ Today, I choose to affirm the great mystery of life eternal, to focus on the Spirit within the body of my beloved. That Spirit lives on.

Suppose you scrub your ethical skin
until it shines,
but inside there is no music,
then what?

KABIR

W ork is a part of my identity but it is not my essence. I have a job I may value, yet I am worthy and interesting without my work. The work of the soul transcends our work in the world. I am a soul engaged on a personal journey. I am a traveler whose unique destination can be reached by many routes. Often apparent detours and reversals bring me to new and important vistas, welcome if unexpected growth. While I value my identity as a worker, I affirm the separate and valued identity of the "I" that does the work. Personal and transcendent, "I" am more than any job I undertake. No one job holds my entire destiny.

Today, I affirm my personal value. I see myself as larger than my job. I recognize my inner dignity separate from my worldly role. I allow my soul to shine, my heart to sing.

People seldom see the halting
and painful steps
by which the most
insignificant success is achieved.

ANNE SULLIVAN

The best solutions rarely come to pass swiftly. Time as well as distance may be necessary to the proper unfolding of events. Choosing to honor the longer view, I surrender my sense of urgency and frustration. I allow life to unfurl as a gentle wave. I do not push for instant satisfaction. Mine is a patient heart. Faced with delays and apparent reversals, I remind myself that my greater good often comes from adversity. Choosing to honor the tidal nature of life, I do not push for artificial solutions born of haste and indiscretion. I allow the universe to unfold with divine timing. I attune myself to the tempo of my highest good.

⊘ Today, I embrace God's timing as my own. Today I place my faith in the divine wisdom that unfolds the seasons each at its proper time. I am a verdant field in the care of universal forces. I allow myself to be nurtured by Divine providence at the proper tempo for my perfect blossoming.

Every instant that the sun is risen,
if I stand in the temple, or on a balcony,
in the hot fields, or in a walled garden,
my own Lord is making love with me.

KABIR

Birth brings me rebirth. My heart expands to encompass new life and new responsibilities. The love of Spirit loves through me, funding me with an abundant flow of gentle affection. I greet the souls that come into my care with tenderness and a sense of adventure. Ours is a shared journey. We are pilgrims traveling together to larger realms. The souls who are my intimates bear gifts for me by their presence. I, too, bear gifts for those I love.

๏ Today, my heart prepares a place for new arrivals. Grounded in Spirit, I am strong, steady and hospitable. A child at heart, I am the welcoming elder to the children that I meet.

It's not the answer that enlightens,
but the question.

EUGENE IONESCO

roblems bear the seeds of their solutions. Beset by worry or anxiety, unable to clearly see my way, I remind myself my soul is connected to all wisdom. I will be led because I am led firmly and certainly whenever I turn within for guidance. In times of adversity, my store of my own inner wisdom may be greater than I know. At such times, I continue to ask for guidance while listening both within and without for the many small signals which help me to find my way. The guidance of Spirit is always available to me if I quiet my anxiety and listen deeply. Answers come to me from many sources. Solutions emerge where questions are posed.

☙ Today, with humility and openness I ask for spiritual intervention in my earthly affairs. I ask for help, and, in the asking, it appears.

Most of us are about as eager
to be changed as we were to be born,
and go through our changes in a similar
state of shock.

JAMES BALDWIN

Transition creates vulnerability. The safety of
the old life has been set aside. The safety of the
new life is not yet in place. The passage between the two feels perilous and threatening. Our feet
move unsteadily on the rope bridge slung across the
jungle chasm and yet, these feelings are illusion. I am
safe and secure at all times, in all situations, however
unsettling. I claim spiritual safety as the bedrock of my
security. My faith is the mountain. Events are the
clouds that hide its face. While it may feel at times that
events have overwhelmed me, I remind myself that
these are passing shadows. My faith endures. My heart,

though vulnerable, is protected. The universe intends me good. Choosing to believe that, I find good in adversity. Elected optimism, while difficult to maintain, is spiritually pragmatic. In opening our hearts to the possibility of good within difficulty, we seize the key of curiosity that allows us to open new doors.

✑ Today, I comfort my threatened heart. I affirm my safety in times of change. I accept the comfort of spiritual sunlight. I am warmed by the truth that I am loved and protected even in the midst of chaotic change. Despite my shock, I survey my new spiritual surroundings with a sense of possibility.

Surviving meant
being born
over and over.

ERICA JONG

&

All beginning is an ending. I both celebrate and grieve. As I choose to start anew in a job, a relationship, a home, I choose to believe in my own resilience. I choose to trust the generosity of life. Calling upon Spirit to supply me, I encounter fulfillment of my wishes, needs and wants. Spirit has abundant supply for my heart's desires. It is the pleasure of Spirit to give. It is my gift back to Spirit to accept. In an antique shop, I find a crystal globe, an antique map that speaks to me of a world lit only by firelight. On a beach, I find the fragile shell washed to me from warmer climes. The falling leaf, vivid and transitory, reminds me of life's cyclicality. A neighbor's wriggling puppy licks my hand. I accept the generosity of Spirit. I allow my life to be made anew.

◌ Today, I embrace the beginning of a better life. I release my grip on the past and open my hand to receive the new. I accept the seeds of the future.

Be strong then,
and enter into your own body;
there you have a solid place for your feet.

K A B I R

⌒

O ur consciousness is independent of our many roles. We define ourselves through work, friendship, family and relationship. When any of these alter we feel cut adrift. "Who am I," I ask, "without . . . ?" Who I am is a child of the entire Universe. My soul has an identity independent of others. My soul has a place that cannot be shaken by external events. Rooted in Spirit, my soul is ever-cherished, ever known and beloved.

⌒ Today, I choose Spirit as the source of my identity. I embrace self-love and self-definition. I am worthy and cherished in changing times.

If you want the truth,
I'll tell you the truth:
Listen to the secret sound, the real sound,
which is inside you.

KABIR

The body is a great teacher. Spirit and body work as a team. In times of bodily illness, I seek spiritual health. I turn within to Spirit, tapping the deep resources of Universal well-being. As I focus on spiritual healing, I experience an undercurrent of wellness that underlies my current experience. As a Spirit, I am healthy. I am vibrant and eternal. Focused on this reality, I gain strength. I gain clarity and resilience. My spiritual energies fund my physical self with support and sustenance.

❧ Today, I focus on the reality that Spirit infuses all of matter and that Spirit is perfect and eternal. I claim the perfect health that is mine as Spirit. I feel myself vibrant and whole.

Our Friendship is made
of being awake.

RUMI

Attention is the gift of solitude. Thrown back on my own resources, deprived of the company of those I love, I learn to cherish my own companionship. As I discover my independence, I also discover my interdependence. I see the gentle and intricate dance of our connection. I perceive the steps I know and the steps I would like to learn. Making good use of my solitude for reflection, I connect deeply to myself, thereby strengthening my capacity to connect with others. I also learn with clarity what it is I love and miss in my companions. Separation teaches both autonomy and connection.

Today, I focus on my relationship to myself. I reach within and make contact with my own spiritual resources. I experience the inner wealth that is mine to share. I connect deeply with myself in preparation for joining with others.

Such is the state of life,
that none are happy but by the
anticipation of change:
the change itself is nothing;
when we have made it, the next wish is
to change again.
The world is not yet exhausted;
let me see something tomorrow
which I never saw before.

SAMUEL JOHNSON

☙

S ometimes it is the seasons in life which are
without drama that are the most challenging.
As life unfolds smoothly but without heightened adrenaline, we experience a sense both of tranquility and loss. We miss a sense of drama that allows
us to define ourselves in terms of our reactions to
outer events. In the absence of dramatic events, we are
asked to turn within and define ourselves. This can feel

frightening, as if we are in an unfamiliar world without landmarks. Who are we in the absence of heightened stress? In peaceful moments, what do we truly desire? The deeper streams of my temperament run strong but quiet. To hear them, I must listen.

℃ Today, I turn my attention to deep inner listening. I attune my spiritual hearing to finer and finer levels as I listen for the subtle ongoing guidance that comes to me in quiet times.

The meeting of two personalities
is like the contact of
two chemical substances:
if there is any reaction, both
are transformed.

C. G. JUNG

Connections are alchemical. Friendships are not static. They are living entities that grow and change. Sometimes my friendships become strained, undergoing mysterious seasons of estrangement. I allow my friendships to alter and grow. I allow them to fall fallow and rest quietly until the season comes for them to bloom again. I do not demand my friendships always be easy. I grant to my friends the freedom to grow, to change, and to challenge me by their altered behaviors and views. I release my friends to their personal trails and timing. I do not take personally their occasional needs for distance and self-containment. My friendships are organic and evolutionary. My friendships are catalytic and transformative. Our intersections spark new growth.

℘ Today, I am flexible and evolutionary. I am a meadow with varied seasons and wealth in each one. I am blessed with abundance and I am abundant in the blessings that I offer to others. The right to change is a blessing that I offer to my friends. We are miners striking new ore at every depth.

The changes in our life
must come from the impossibility
to live otherwise
than according to the demands
of our conscience.

LEO TOLSTOY

☙

Each of us has an inner compass. Its voice calls us to our highest good. Sometimes it requires that we alter a longstanding but stifling situation. It is difficult to face the severing or alteration of a relationship even when we know such change is for the highest good. Faced with a divorce or separation, faced with the need to terminate a long-standing friendship, I must remind myself that sometimes the most loving involvement is a non-involvement. It is tempting, always, to try to go back, to hold onto what once was rather than face what that relationship has now become. I resolve with a loving heart to accept appropriate endings. I do not grasp at straws when the reality is difficult but clear. Instead, I release the past, bless it and turn with resolution to the future. I listen to the dictates of my conscience, knowing that its voice calls me home.

℘ Today, I place my humbled heart in universal care, asking for healing and direction.

Let the great world spin
for ever down
the ringing grooves of change.

LORD TENNYSON

☙

The world is a forest of verdant possibility. No one person controls my happiness. No one person is the source of my joy. I am rooted in universal flow. My needs for love and affection are met by many sources. I am blessed by the ability to receive love through many channels. I open my heart to the love that is offered to me by multiple sources. My heart is a mountain meadow fed by many streams.

☙ Today, I practice receptivity to loving forces. At any moment, a divinely inspired intersection may occur. I accept the good which flows to me from many sides.

Nothing that grieves us
can be called little:
by the eternal laws of proportion
a child's loss of a doll
and a king's loss of a crown are
events of the same size.

MARK TWAIN

All risk risks rejection. The sting of criticism can create a spiral of shame. Bitten by shame, it is easy to become embittered, to shrink back from life and slide toward despair. I do not allow myself this dangerous luxury. Faced with hostility I turn within for spiritual comfort, reminding myself I am a child of the Universe, worthy of love, care and respect. Aware of my vulnerability, I treat myself gently with the same care I would extend to an injured friend. My dignity is grounded in my spiritual identity. I hold my worth in the face of hostility. I am unshaken by the sting of personal assault. I allow my heart to be a fortress. My spirit is like the face of a mountain proud and bright in the sun.

℃ Today, I stand firm in my own worthiness. My dignity is solid and enduring. My faith is the rock on which I build my life. I dare to risk and I risk my daring. I am large enough to survive my losses and enjoy my gains.

Though lovers be lost love shall not;
And death shall have no dominion.

DYLAN THOMAS

൭

We rely on those we love to be our sounding boards. Their perceptions and opinions are part of what we love. When we lose our loved ones, we do not lose their interactions with us. Instead, we are asked to listen more acutely for the guidance that they offer. This guidance may come to us as intuition. It may come to us as memory. It may come to us as friends and strangers speaking to us in the tone of our lost love. As we open our hearts to continued relationship with those who have passed on, we find ourselves helped at many turns, protected in many ways. Our loved ones continue to love us as we do them. As we open our hearts and our minds to their continued love, we are reminded by a sense of their presence.

C&æ Today, I allow myself to be aided and guided by those who have gone before. Just as the mighty tree springs from the tiny seed, my full flowering is rooted in all that have gone before me. I celebrate the continuity of life. I am part of a larger whole and it is a part of me.

Stop the words now.
Open the window in the center
of your chest,
and let the spirits fly in and out.

RUMI

In our lives, we are many sizes, experiencing ourselves as both large and small. Often a change for
the better can cause us to actually feel worse. We
doubt our worthiness of the good that has come our
way. We temporarily feel small, out of our depth, off-
center. Our dreams are coming true and we do not feel
large enough to inhabit them. We shrink back in the
face of the life we have created. In such times of self-
diminishment, I remind myself: I am the flower of
God. My life blossoms through God. The good which
comes to me is God's business, not my own. When I al-

· 61 ·

low my life to open and bloom, I am allowing God to find expression in the world.

☙ Today, I surrender my resistance to being large. I allow God to choose my size for me.

*True friendship is a plant
of slow growth,
and must undergo and withstand
the shocks of adversity
before it is entitled to the appellation.*

GEORGE WASHINGTON

F riendships require honesty and honesty requires courage. In all friendships there are moments when we must choose to be courageous.
Our friendships have become root-bound and so must
be repotted, transplanted and transformed into a
larger and healthier vessel. This transition requires us
to speak the difficult truth. Speaking our hearts' truth,
while not always easy, yields us the bedrock on which
the friendship stands firm. As I choose to speak with
integrity and openness, I commit more deeply both to
myself and to others. As I learn to trust the safety of

open communication, I find that I open like a plant responding to the sun. Honesty is healing and nutritious to my heart and its friendships.

CB Today, I blossom in honesty and openness. Today, I allow the nutrition of honest communication to foster my relationships to greater health.

The sun sets and the moon sets,
but they're not gone. *Death is*
a coming together.

RUMI

❧

Death is both dramatic and subtle. Over time, the parting of a loved one becomes less harsh as slowly and gently a continued bond is revealed. As I open my heart to the promptings and guidance of those I love who have passed from the physical sphere, I am alert to the contact which comes to me in many forms—as memory, as intuition and coincidence. Rather than bitterly close my heart, I allow myself to maintain a gentle but alert attention to the touch of Spirit. I remind myself that life begets life and that those I love live on in my loving memory of them. I also allow for the possibility that my memory lives on in them, triggering their concerned contact in subtle forms.

⌘ Today, I deliberately practice open-mindedness. I cultivate a willingness to experience subtle realms.

Fortunately psychoanalysis
is not the only way
to resolve inner conflicts.
Life itself still remains a very
effective therapist.

KAREN HORNEY

❦

In daily life there is an inner transition I can consciously practice. This is the transition from fear to faith. Faced with ambiguity and uncertainty, I can choose to believe things will work out for the best. The lost job will yield me a new and better one. The difficult friendship set aside yields room for new friends to enter. The novel direction taken by my current thought will prove fruitful, not merely eccentric. All is working toward the good. Rather than indulge in worry and second-guessing, I can elect to believe there is wisdom in the unfolding of events exactly as they are. For many, the decision to switch from fear to faith is a decision to switch from pessimism to optimism. As we choose to be open-minded and optimistic about our lives, we are graced with an alert attention to our own unfolding good. I am a witness to my own miraculous growth.

☙ Today, I choose conscious optimism. My life is God's field planted with the seeds of my future blossoming.

To keep a lamp burning
we have to keep
putting oil in it.

MOTHER TERESA

ommunication is often difficult. Friendships
may become clouded by unspoken and un-
shared feelings. In times when my friendships
are shadowed by such secrecy, I remind myself that I
can hold a bright lamp in my heart, waiting for the
right time to gently clear the air. Listening with an inner ear for the proper moment to present itself, I resolve to bravely but softly share my feelings, thoughts
and insights. Rather than harbor anger or resentment
when communication is stifled, I pray for the well-
being of my estranged friend, communicating on a
spiritual level my continued commitment to our bond.

⚘ Today, I renew my inner commitment to honesty. Today, I listen for right timing for when to speak my heart. Alert and willing to follow inner guidance, I choose my moment and my words with healing grace.

Everything is so dangerous
that nothing
is really very frightening.

GERTRUDE STEIN

ა

As we travel, we change cultures and consciousness. Our sense of self may be both heightened and shaky. Traveling, I am opened to
new outer vistas and new inner perspectives. I am
taught to view life from a higher angle, to gain a sense
of my placement against a broader canvas. We are travelers at all times, although we seldom view life as the
journey that it is. Traveling, I gain a sense of my personal trajectory. I take stock, measuring my progress
toward perceived goals. Freed from the ordinary structure of my life, I am freed, too, to evaluate that life, to
ascertain whether its outer form matches my inner

needs. Life can be led in myriad ways. Viewing my many options, I select my own favored path.

⟡ Today, I view myself as a pilgrim. I take stock of the distances I have traveled. I take time to map the route I now choose.

Sickness sensitizes
man for observation,
like a photographic plate.

EDMOND AND JULES DE GONCOURT

Illness shocks us body and soul. Its suffering forces us into new territory. While we are often unable to find a cause for our disease, we are often moved to greater spiritual opening. As well as the bitter fruits of pain and trauma, we harvest the more subtle gifts of openness and acceptance. As we face the challenge of an illness striking unfairly and without warning, we also inventory the richness of the life that it interrupts. We may discover we have lived fully, lovingly and well. We may realize the depth of the bonds with those we cherish. Sudden and catastrophic illness is a spiritual trapdoor that plummets us into the net of the Universe. In our free fall, we often discover surprising faith and acceptance. We are ambushed into our spiritual health.

☙ Today, I find health in my illness. Today, I find well-being at the core of my dis-ease. I accept the condition unexpectedly thrust upon me. With this new land-mark, I find my spiritual bearings and greater growth.

The call of death is a call of love.
Death can be sweet if we answer it
in the affirmative,
if we accept it as one of the great eternal
forms of life and transformation.

HERMANN HESSE

There are no compassionate words strong enough to hold our suffering hearts in the face of death. It is the loving intention beneath the words, running through them, that forms the net for our falling hearts. Even as we tumble to the depths of despair, we are caught in the net of compassion. There are those who love us as we have loved. There are those who have suffered loss as we do. Every love is unique and individual. Every loss is personal and particular. Yet the great web of life embraces one and all. Our suffering is a known suffering. Our healing is an eventuality toward which all the Universe tends. As we enter the portals of grief, we are met by the understanding of the ages. Birth, love and death are landmarks of the human condition. As I open my heart to accept the reality of a beloved's passing, I open my heart to my own humanity. Rather than isolate myself, feeling somehow special in my grief, I choose to see that my sorrow is the sorrow of the ages—poignant, personal and particular, yet universal in nature.

CS Today, I accept my tears of grief as the life-giving rain that fosters new growth. Even in the face of death itself, I feel the resiliency of life moving me inexorably onward to greater good.

When the mind becomes quiet,
you feel nourished.

SWAMI CHIDVILASANANDA

᭪

Some seasons are less colorful than others. Temperate, even boring, such times require we creatively seek our own diversions. The soul has many weathers. In times of calm, I remind myself that growth occurs slowly and steadily. When I am tempted to artificially stir up drama in my environment, I remind myself that drama often diverts deeper and more substantial growth. My heart is a serene woodland lake. The winds of change ripple it lightly.

᭪ Today, I allow subtlety in my own unfolding. I value serenity. I cherish peace.

*Change is not made
without inconvenience.*

RICHARD HOOKER

❧

Change creates friction and friction creates change. As we welcome the new, we must surrender the old. Our developing life requires that we make room for it. As we sort papers, clean drawers and clear closets, we are ordering far more than our physical life. As we create harmony, we attract harmony. Our lives become sweeter, less chaotic, more flowing. Clearing away the physical blocks to a serene environment, I clear away the psychic blocks to personal serenity. Change, however inconvenient, creates convenience and flow.

❧ Today, I am a clear stream flowing softly through green meadows. I make my way swiftly but gently to my goals.

Let that which stood in front go behind,
Let that which was behind advance
to the front.

WALT WHITMAN

☙

Loss transforms perspective. The pain of loss can be staggering. Struck down by grief and longing, it is difficult to cope and more difficult to imagine life regaining sweetness. In seasons of mourning, care must be taken. We must consciously and creatively choose to fill our days with gentle good. This means we must focus our attention on the present moment, scanning its particular delights even if from an emotional distance. The cat in the window. The geranium blooming on a sill. The golden retriever bounding at its owner's side. Each of these singular sights can touch the frozen heart, gently waking it to new life even amidst pain. In severe seasons of heartache we are asked to protect and care for ourselves like vulnerable children taking a childlike delight in the tiny joys of life.

✑ Today, I choose to cherish myself like a beloved child. I treat myself gently and with compassion. Practicing alert attention, I find delight in the small treasures of the day. I allow meaningful moments to assume enhanced perspective. Counting these blessings, I enrich my impoverished heart.

Help your brother's boat across,
and lo! your own has reached the shore.

HINDU PROVERB

The world is an ocean of possibility. Relationships deepen and alter. As we move beyond our accustomed depth, new attitudes and shells are required. It is like learning to swim. The water will support us if we learn to allow it. So, too, in relationships, we must develop the faith necessary to float as well as to strive. Just as a swimmer must learn to trust the waters that hold him, we must learn to trust that the relationship can support the weight of our personality. Rather than constant effort we must relax and allow ourselves to trust the subtle energies of love. All relationships require vulnerability. As I learn to open to this fact, I soften into a flexible strength.

Today, I practice faith in my unfolding relationship. Like an autumn leaf borne on the wind, I allow myself to be carried gently forward.

ℭ

Physical change invites spiritual change. Our physical bodies are the vehicles that carry us through life. As we alter our physical appearance, our interactions with others are also affected. Time and compassion are required to adjust to shifts in our personal appearance. A gain or loss of weight, a new hairstyle or color, a shift in clothing—any of these may open the door to feelings of vulnerability, even fragility. Conversely, as we strengthen our bodies, we may feel the power of our own magnetism, the energy of our sexuality, the gift of our own attractive nature. I remind myself life is seasonal and that as my appearance alters, I am moving through a shift which

I will weather with grace, dignity, even humor. My "changing look" alters my outlook. I accept the expanded vision that comes to me as a gift of my altered self.

    ☙ Today, I treat myself with compassion. I embrace my altered persona and I accept the many changes that it brings.

Love doesn't just sit there like a stone,
it has to be made,
like brick; re-made all the time,
made new.

URSULA K. LeGUIN

I build my friendships with the conscious architecture of my integrity. My design contains space for change. My friendships are flexible and resilient. I do not demand that my relationships remain static and unvarying. Instead, I allow my bonds to be mutable and varied. At times I am close and at times I am more distant from even my closest friends. Such is the natural tide of relationships. I accept the changing tides of my friendships. I allow flow and mutability. My heart is a spiritual shoreline with intricate tides that I honor and respect.

☙ Today, I respect the changing garden of my life. I focus on those areas that are in blossom and I allow other areas to lie fallow knowing they, too, will blossom in their turn.

Often God shuts a door
in our face,
And then subsequently opens the door
through which we need to go.

CATHERINE MARSHALL

The heart is more daring and resilient than we often imagine. Faced with the grief of a relationship altering, we often feel both unloved and unloving, as if we have exhausted our capacity for love. There is a larger truth. We are immersed in love, a part of love and a portal for love to love through us. Reminding myself I am loved by divine love and able to love through divine love, I allow my heart to soften and dissolve its wounding. I allow my heart to open into compassion. Loving myself through the conscious acceptance of my vulnerability, I embrace my ability to transform and transcend.

❧ Today, I allow the alchemy of divine love to transform a difficult ending into a new beginning. My heart is a phoenix and today I celebrate its flight.

Courage is the price
that life exacts
for granting peace.

AMELIA EARHART

⁓

Sometimes our lives are torn asunder. The tornado of change comes to us swiftly and seemingly without mercy. What was, is no longer. We are cast adrift. The fabric of our existence is torn end to end. Even in times of such extreme transition, there is an underlying working toward the good. Even in times in which grief blinds us, in which we rage against our fate, there is a tide that can move us toward growth and healing.

⁓ Today, I consciously and deliberately soften my heart against bitterness. I ask the healing grace of universal love to comfort me and draw me to new beginnings. I choose to release from my heart its bitter trauma and its shock. I accept the deeper growth I am offered through my terrible sorrow. I open my heart by asking for universal forces to aid me in my time of need.

There is a Secret One inside us;
the planets in all the galaxies
pass through his hands like beads.

That is a string of beads one should look
at with luminous eyes.

KABIR

We are like jewelers. At the start of any day, we have before us the beautiful beads of differing choices. Choice by choice, moment by moment, I build the necklace of my day, stringing together the choices that form artful living. Will I be quiet today or outgoing, solitary or involved with friends, reflective or expressive? Will I write letters, make phone calls, pay bills, sweep floors or go for a good long walk? Moving through my days with conscious grace, I connect to the web of life. I, too, am a bead in a larger pattern.

✑ Today, I choose to live by conscious design, nurturing myself and others in body, mind and spirit. I ask for and receive guidance in my choices. I cherish the pattern of my life.

We can never go back again,
that much is certain.

DAPHNE DU MAURIER

Sometimes people fail us in terrible ways. We are betrayed, abandoned, cast aside. In times of such personal trauma, we must hold to the larger picture. The Universe does not betray us. The Universe does not leave our side. Even in the midst of grievous loss, we are led and comforted. We are cared for and protected. Although I may fail to see it, a higher hand operates in my affairs. I realize that while people may indeed fail me and turn away, there is an underlying goodness to the Universe which brings to me new friends and new situations. These gifts heal and soothe me. I see the merciful hand of providence despite my pain.

Today, I place my trust in universal love. I open my heart to receive care and comfort from unexpected sources. I allow my good to come from many quarters. I surrender my fixed ideas as to what best serves me. I open to the innovative grace of my unfolding life.

One is happy as a result
of one's own efforts, once one
knows the necessary ingredients
of happiness—simple tastes,
a certain degree of courage,
self-denial to a point,
love of work, and above all,
a clear conscience.
Happiness is no vague dream,
of that I now feel certain.

GEORGE SAND

H appiness is a by-product of right living. Right action leads us to right thinking. In some seasons, we are able to act decisively in directions that please us and feel happiness as a result. At other times, life is less linear and more variable. Happiness is more elusive as we experience events and timing beyond our control. Among life's vivid seasons, there are also times of a more muffled love, periods of muted mood and ambivalent, even ambiguous feelings. These are the limbo times, the gray days that fall in between. These are the transitional times when I am not what I was nor am yet what I am becoming. In limbo times, I must live with alert attention to my feelings of vulnerability. I must guard against hasty choices and rushed decisions. In limbo times I must learn to simply be. Soon enough life will move me onward.

 Ɂ Today, I practice the action of loving non-action. I allow my life to alter organically and without unnatural haste. I trust the tempo of my unfolding.

Thinkers, listen, tell me
what you know of that is not
inside the soul?

K A B I R

The heart has dreams and hopes it hides from public view. The heart has secret sorrows, private woes. Listening to my heart, I must listen with gentle ears. If I judge too harshly, my heart will not speak of disappointments and their pain will remain. My heart requires my tenderness to speak its secrets. My heart rewards my love by being the true compass by which I may steer my life.

Today, my heart is safe within my keeping. I offer my heart compassionate ears to hear its dreams.

When people make changes in their lives
in a certain area,
they may start by changing
the way they talk about that subject,
how they act about it,
their attitude toward it,
or an underlying decision concerning it.

JANE ILLSLEY CLARK

N ew skills lend sparkle to our lives. Hobbies enrich the soul. The piano learned for joy, the handmade sweater knit for a cherished niece, the newly painted kitchen chair—these actions light our daily lives. A small simple homely poem, a pot of soup, a brightly colored leaf pressed into a book—these are the beautiful stones my home is built upon. I can accomplish some beauty in every day. I can add to my world by my artfulness.

∂ Today, I act in small and concrete ways to bring beauty to my home. I allow the hand of the Great Creator to work through me, bringing grace and order to my surroundings.

It is change,
continuing change,
inevitable change,
that is the dominant factor
in society today.

ISAAC ASIMOV

Sometimes we are faced with events beyond our control. Our friends accept jobs in distant cities. The one we love falls suddenly and irrevocably in love with someone else. Our company downsizes. A fire sweeps our neighborhood and our house is lost in flames. Faced with such losses, our hearts are seized by fear. We feel swept beyond our depth, adrift in a dangerous sea. The world appears a hostile and forbidding place. We are frightened. At times like these, we draw into ourselves, contracting our hearts self-protectively. It is a natural reflex—and it is counter to our good. In times of adversity, we must expand, not contract. We must open, not close. We must open our hand to receive aid rather than clutch tightly to what we have remaining.

  Today, I let go. I release my defenses. Rather than hold myself tightly curled into the fist I use to fight adversity, I open my heart's hand to allow the touch of friendship, the touch of hope. Rather than harden my heart against further blows, I soften it to receive new beginnings.

You must do the thing
you think you cannot do.

ELEANOR ROOSEVELT

 С₿

Optimism in the face of uncertainty is a difficult art. The terrain of life is varied and mysterious. I cannot always see the path ahead.
At times my view is shadowed by doubt, constricted by
fear. The open vistas of optimism are closed to me. In
such shortsighted times, I must practice the discipline
of positive attitudes. I must consciously choose to expect a benevolent future despite my shaken faith.
Grounded in the routine of each day's unfolding business, I must act in alignment with my coming good.
This means I say "yes" to opportunities for new adventures and acquaintances to enter my life. I say "yes"
to unexpected doors opening. Rather than cling to my

known life, I allow that life to alter and expand. I choose to take positive risk. I step out in faith despite my misgivings.

ᢙ Today, I open my mind and heart to the new vistas before me. I embrace change and accept unfolding possibilities. I am a fertile field available for God's planting.

The things that have
come into being
change continually.

AUGUSTO ROA BASTOS

s we move to embrace new vistas, we are not asked to abandon those we love. As life leads me forward—to a new job, a new home, a new relationship—I do not need to close my heart to all that has gone before. My heart is a worthy vessel. It carries riches gained from my living adventures. It carries room enough for other riches to be gathered. I move through life like a trader, bringing gifts to those I meet and leaving their sides enriched by the gifts they bear for me. Life is always bountiful, always adventurous, if I will open my heart to the new lands being of-

fered. As a spiritual sailor, I must lift the sail of faith
and allow destiny's wind to move me forward.

♔ Today, I welcome the winds of change. Today I cooperate with the new experiences coming to my soul.

&

We often speak of desiring "sound" lives without realizing how telling the phrase is. By focusing on the sound of my life, I can alter and improve my life. What is the tone of my voice? What is the tone of my environment? As I focus on the "pitch" of my life, I can create harmony. My voice, the music I choose, even the tone of my prayers—all these factors contribute to my life's being "sound."

& Today, I live gently and harmoniously. Today, I voice praise, gratitude and healing.

All that is necessary
to make this world a better place
to live is to love——to love as
Christ loved, as Buddha loved.

ISADORA DUNCAN

We do not interact at random. We are in
each other's lives for spiritual reasons. We
have "business" with one another. By consciously choosing to focus on why I have met someone,
on how I can best serve and expand another, I bring to
each encounter a heightened awareness. As I ask to love
all and serve all, I bring forward my spiritual gifts and
call forward the gifts of others. Grace fills every moment when we are truly present. Sometimes we transit
each other's lives like benevolent planets.

Today, I ask to be a loving and expansive presence for those whom I meet. I offer myself as a loving conduit for the goodness of the Universe to move through me, blessing all I encounter.

Spiritual power can be seen
in a person's reverence
for life—hers and all others,
including animals and nature,
with a recognition of a universal
life force referred to by
many as God.

VIRGINIA SATIR

Cᕒᕒ

Unity charges all of life. One energy connects us all, linking us soul to soul and heart to heart. At any time, in any place, I can go within and feel my connection to all of life. As spiritual beings, we are vast and mysterious. The heart is generous and capacious. The heart is far-reaching and all-inclusive. The heart can contain far-flung loves. The heart can love despite geography.

Today, my heart holds all my beloveds close despite the distance between us. Today my heart is full of connections, alive with the knowledge of the tender web which holds us all in its embrace.

&

My heart is a tiny town welcoming those who enter. I can choose to be open or closed to those whom I meet, and so, I choose to be open. My attitude determines the caliber of our interactions. As I consciously choose a welcoming heart, I bring to the world a place where dynamic and healing interactions can occur. I am a single soul, yet that soul is a bright lantern. I become medicine for all I encounter. I, too, am healed by the balm of an open heart. Rather than diminish my importance by saying "I am only one," I choose instead to be a useful instrument in the unfolding of a better world. I consciously align myself with the highest good, asking always to be guided and empowered. In my family, my business and my community I work to make this earth a better place. Mine is a hospitable heart.

℘ Today, I greet life with openness, wonder and curiosity. I offer respectful interest and attention to all. I salute the wisdom, dignity and grace of those whom I encounter.

It is good to have an end
to journey towards;
but it is the journey that matters,
in the end.

URSULA K. LeGUIN

M y life is fruitful and abundant. Just as
the earth has its cycles and seasons, so,
too, our own lives have times of planting,
times of growth and times of harvest. So much of my
frustration comes from my refusal to accept life's seasons as they come to me. An adolescent child enters a
period of rebellion. This is necessary to full maturation. A project at the midpoint is sprawling and un-
wieldy. This, too, is necessary. A marriage enters a time
of solo growth and trajectories as each partner pursues
independent interests. However unsettling, this, too, is
healthy. Not all seasons lie serene in the sun, yet each

has its place. As I ask to be attuned to life's cycles, I feel my anxiety slipping away. I rest in the faith that all is unfolding according to right timing. I am where I should be when I should be. I am alert to the good of every moment.

CSS Today, I accept divine timing. I allow the pacing of the Universe to be my own. I align myself with the tempo of my life precisely as it is unfolding.

If you want the truth,
I will tell you the truth:
Friend, listen: the God whom I love
is inside.

KABIR

ᏨᎬ

One life, one love, one energy runs through all
of creation. This Life is Spirit, an inner river
that can be tapped into at any time. Knowing this, we are divinely guided at all times. In any
place, in any circumstance, the Inner Voice has clarity
and direction for me, if I will seek it out. Often it is
just an act of focusing that brings the sense of direction more fully into play. When outward events jostle
me with their velocity and turbulence, I must actively
turn within, seeking higher perceptions.

⊗ Today, I release the urgency of outer events. I listen to the inner rhythm of God. I set my pace by divine guidance. The world and its busy agendas do not control my soul. My soul rests in God: good, orderly direction.

Life is measured
by the rapidity of change.

GEORGE ELIOT

❧

L ife is often turbulent. The rapids and eddies of
the day's events may pull at our consciousness
like tiny hands. Beneath the turbulence of daily
living, there is a longer, slower pulse of perfect timing.
It is to that rhythm that I give my soul. I listen beneath
the turbulence of daily life. I open myself to the guidance of higher forces. I ask for and receive adjustments
in my priorities. I allow myself to find the tempo most
attuned to my personal unfolding.

❧ Today, I act and react with a sense of the larger
view, the truer goals. I give myself assurance that God's
timing is my own and serves my own best interests.

Most of the change we think
we see in life
Is due to truths being in
and out of favor.

ROBERT FROST

We are evolutionary and revolutionary. As we grow and evolve, our inner identities shift. Sometimes outer circumstances move more slowly. Old forms and images mask the emerging truth. When that happens, we are often frustrated, feeling that people do not see us for who we truly are. At such times patience and communication are key. I must give people both the time and the information necessary to know me anew. In my friendships, I must marshall an alert attention, seeing others with a fresh eye as they, too, change and evolve. The truth of who we are and who our friends are must allow for the possibility of continual redefinition. Respect for the changes in myself and others deepens and enriches the garden of friendship.

℥ Today, I take the time to get my friends and acquaintances current on the shifts in my inner life. I communicate clearly and openly. I allow time for people to adjust to the ways in which I have changed. I, too, adjust to the change in others.

Whatever you receive,
wherever it comes from,
cherish the desire to give it back
in full measure.

SWAMI CHIDVILASANANDA

❧

Sometimes, even in the midst of a busy and crowded life, we are pierced by loneliness. We long to be understood, to feel a sense of deep and enduring companionship. If only, we think, I had someone with whom I could share myself internally, on all levels. If only I had a true companion . . . At these times, we must look to the ways we are always perfectly partnered, carefully and deeply guarded and guided by the Universe itself. The Universe never abandons us. There is always a perfect partnering, a constant and continual reaching out to each of us.

Today, I remind myself that despite my loneliness I am not alone. I turn my attention to the unique partnering that comes to me from many quarters. I accept the companionship of an interactive Universe. I am with friends.

With an eye made quiet by the power
Of harmony, and the deep power of joy,
We see into the life of things.

WILLIAM WORDSWORTH

Modern life can feel dangerous and unstable. Removed from a sense of natural unfolding, our lives can seem precarious and chaotic. Both business and busy-ness can distract us from realizing the deeper flow. We may feel only the rapids and not the nurturing waters. In times of such stress and anxiety, I seek a foundation firmer than the choppy flow of external events. Like a tree buffeted by the wind, I am yet grounded in the deep soil of my spiritual life. My roots are strong and self-nurturing. They draw to me sustenance and support.

◌ Today, I root myself in the earth. I connect to the seasons and cycles of life, the great wheel of nature that sustains us all. I reach beneath my daily life, funding my soul with the grace that underlies all things. I am grounded in life itself.

*No trumpets sound
when the important decisions
of our life are made.
Destiny is made known silently.*

AGNES DeMILLE

L ife is verdant and generous despite times of
drought, doubt and despair. New beginnings
are subtle and in my pain and impatience I can
often overlook the shoots of fresh growth tenaciously
winning through even in difficult times. It takes an
alert attention to recognize and appreciate my small
gains in seasons of adversity. I choose to consciously
focus on the gently growing good. As I choose to see
my progress I can offer myself honor for my tenacity,
my resilience and my faith.

Today, I open my eyes to my own gentle progress. I recognize and salute my courage. I applaud my small gains and offer myself compassion for being a work in progress.

We tend to think of the rational
as a higher order,
but it is the emotional
that makes our lives.
One often learns more from
ten days of agony
than from ten years of contentment.

MERLE SHAIN

S ometimes change is sudden and catastrophic. Life as we know it is abruptly overturned. We have an earthquake of the heart so severe that the landscape will never look the same. In times of sudden chaos, the soul finds its ground in the eternal. It turns instinctively toward God, even if it uses other names. An acute listening takes hold as the soul attunes itself to hear more deeply. This deeper listening is an automatic response as natural as breathing.

⚓ Today, I listen with my deepest heart. I am alert and responsive to guidance in many forms and formats. As I open my attention to a broad range of cues, I find myself guided and guarded. My heart is anchored in spiritual seas. Storms rise and pass yet I survive.

. . . that is what learning is.
You suddenly understand
something you've understood all your life,
but in a new way.

DORIS LESSING

ॐ

A change in perception can be as radical as turning on the lights in a darkened room. Suddenly we see what we could not see before. Our eyes are opened. Our necessary path becomes clear. Such breakthroughs into clarity can be shocking, even painful. What I now see is an uncomfortable truth. I must change to accommodate my unsparing vision. I must accept what I have long denied. In times of such poignant awakening, I must be patient and gentle with my startled self. Clarity is the bedrock of an honest life. That foundation is what I am building.

ᐉ Today, I gently and resolutely face difficult truths. I open my eyes to facing that which I have found un-faceable. Remembering that sight brings insight, I invite the sunlight of the spirit to illuminate my life.

My lifetime listens
to yours.

MURIEL RUKEYSER

⌘

The world is peopled by travelers each with a
journey. As we make our way through our own
obstacles, we are often oblivious to those who
travel by our side. And yet when we open our hearts to
the adventures and adversities of others, our own journey is illumined. Those who travel beside me are my
teachers and those I teach in turn.

⌘ Today, I turn my attention to the lives of others. I
open to the interactive dance of our intersecting lives.
Alert and attentive, I learn from those around me. Em-
pathetic and involved, I teach what I have learned.
Ours is a journey of shared hearts. I lift the lantern of
camaraderie.

Imagination has always had powers
of resurrection
that no science can match.

INGRID BENGIS

☙

M uch of modern life is stressful and ca-
cophonous. It is both chaotic and disturb-
ing in the frequent turbulence and velocity
of change. Maintaining a sense of calm and even flow
is an elusive goal that is attained through gently maintaining a spiritual practice amidst the hubbub of our
secular lives. Spiritual practice is central to my sense of
well-being. Nothing takes precedence over my soul's
unfolding. I take the time and make the effort to touch
base with myself on a spiritual level throughout the
day.

Today, I take time to practice spiritual deepening. Setting aside a few moments for quiet contemplation, I turn my attention inward to a calm center in my heart. There, in the meadow of stillness, I pause to refresh my spirit.

Man's yesterday may ne'er be like
his morrow;
Nought may endure but Mutability.

PERCY BYSSHE SHELLEY

☙

Elders walk before us. The young follow behind.
Ours is a caravan of consciousness. The sands
of Spirit shift beneath our feet as we trudge
together toward a future we are all of us making. Ours
is an elective and a collective adventure. We add to the
whole by our conscious participatory humanity. Each
of us is important. Each indispensable. As I choose to
act and interact, kindly and generously, my world becomes a kinder and more generous world.

☙ Today, I embrace the longer view. I see my place in
the great scheme of human events.

What most of us want
is to be heard,
to communicate.

DORY PREVIN

hen we are engaged deeply with others, our changes often come to us as a result of theirs. When a spouse or child sustains a stunning loss, we, too, feel it. When a loved one achieves heady success, their fearful giddy uncertainty, painful insecurity or jubilant grandiosity becomes ours to deal with. Even rooted as we are in our own individuality, nonetheless we live in community and commiseration with those we love. Often our love is a shelter when they are in need. We sometimes serve as much as a loving place as a person.

❧ Today, I am rooted in my own life but I offer shade and shelter to those I love. I am responsive, not merely reactive to their needs and wants. I open my heart to carry their hearts and dreams within my own. I am large enough to care about the small things which loom large to others.

ငၵ

The advent of a new life brings a new birth to our consciousness as well. We step into new shoes, walking with greater care and consciousness as we shepherd a new life among us. We are born many times in each lifetime. As we choose to be remade as a nurturing elder, we take on qualities which accrue to this new role. We find ourselves patient, doting, delighted at small steps. As we embrace a newborn, we open to new dimensions in ourselves. We become nurturing caretakers to the child without and the child within as we accept the invitation to love and laugh, to cry and care, to nourish and nurture the soul adventuring forth in our midst.

◌ Today, I commit to new love. I open my heart to its arrival. I welcome the child who makes me an elder and remember the elder child who is me.

People need joy.
Quite as much as clothing.
Some of them need it far more.

MARGARET COLLIER GRAHAM

℘

nimals love us with constant hearts. They offer us pure joy, a place to love with simplicity
and purity. In caring for our pets, we structure our lives. Their regular needs become our soothing
habits. We walk the dog but the dog walks us. Adding
a pet to our lives adds richness and warmth. Losing a
pet, we lose an irreplaceable friend, the companion of
fond memories. Our pets are both our wealth and our
witnesses. They sweetly and softly gentle our days.

℘ Today, I cherish my animal companions. I count
myself fortunate for the time spent in their presence. I
savor the connection of life to life and love to love. I
celebrate the bond of our affection.

Ꮛ

We are not defined or limited by the things which we own but we do cherish certain belongings and the pleasure they bring to our lives. A fine car, a nicely balanced pen, the crystal paperweight catching the sun, the needlepoint pillow, the delicate vase, the favorite coffee mug—all these things partner us through our days, comforting us with their cozy sameness. The loss of a cherished object—the broken teacup from Grandmother, the favorite sweater lost at the cleaners—can sadden and haunt us. Our sense of continuity teeters and we grieve.

Today, I appreciate the flow of beautiful objects through my life. I take time to honor the associations they hold for me. I pause and remember the circumstances they evoke for me. I savor their place in my passage.

You need only claim
the events of your life
to make yourself yours.

FLORIDA SCOTT-MAXWELL

We alter our lives by the opinions we hold of them. If we see ourselves as daring, we will dare. We can change our lives by changing our perceptions. We can identify those plots and patterns we wish to alter. While it is important to have the faculty of self-scrutiny, it is equally important to have the gift of self-appreciation. We can identify and cherish those character traits which are our strengths. I acknowledge and appreciate my own accomplishments and talents. I note when I do well and applaud myself for my merits. Such self-appraisal is not mere narcissism. It is the bedrock of solid self-worth.

᎒ Today, I take a positive inventory of my assets. I count and consider my own virtues. I notice what I value and I build upon those values. I become the person I choose to be.

You could not step twice into
the same rivers;
for other waters are ever flowing
on to you.

HERACLITUS

☙

The world is vast and variable. Just as our diet must be varied and succulent for optimum health, so too the rhythms of our days must have variety and altered tempos so we can appreciate the musicality of life.

☙ Today, I consciously pace my day. I pay alert attention to the tempo of life's unfolding. I enjoy the pulse of life, the vitality of action and the peace of repose. "Rest" is a musical term and I savor the quiet moments of my day, the subtle seasons of my life as well as those times fraught with drama and urgency. I am a symphony of many moods. I accept them all.

One writes a novel in order to know
why one writes.
It's the same with life—you live not
for some end,
but in order to know why you live.

ALBERTO MORAVIA

L ife is a constant and patient teacher. Lessons come to us and return to us for our greater mastery. As we acknowledge and appreciate our gains, we minimize our losses. Focusing on our strengths, our weaknesses slip away as we build on a bedrock of right action. All lives are a mixture of gain and loss. As I choose to acknowledge the negative while focusing on the positive, I acquire a steadfast foothold of reality. Allowing for improvement while not expecting perfection, I am a work in progress. By embracing a willingness to learn as well as an attention to lessons learned already, I find myself both healthy and humble. I am right-sized and right-minded. A resilient optimism holds sway.

✍ Today, I choose to practice alert attention to the lessons life is teaching. I consciously strive to see my options and choose wisely. I avoid the pitfalls of the past. I act decisively yet with discretion. I am a student of life.

Change begets change.
Nothing propagates so fast.

CHARLES DICKENS

A bountiful life mixes continuity and change. We rest secure in our past while we add in the elements of our future. Sometimes change sweeps in on us from outside but more often we set change in motion through our own gardening hand. We take the beginner's lessons which blossom into a burgeoning skill. We empty the bulging closets to make way for the new. As I focus on each day, taking the small and appropriate actions necessary to its best unfolding, I am building the larger movements of my life. As in music, large changes are wrought by tiny notes.

Today, I appreciate what I have while I add in small notes of what I want. I cherish the continuity of friends, work and interests while I seek the leavening of new people and novel activities. I allow change to come both to me and through me. I am rooted in the old while I am open to the new.

We are shaped
and fashioned
by what we love.

JOHANN WOLFGANG VON GOETHE

☙

Desire is a compass for our lives' directions. As we become clear in what we want, as we allow ourselves to yearn, we become conduits for the Universe to act upon us and through us. My desire is a prayer impressed on the heart of God. My openness is the willingness to receive. My courage is the faith to act on what I receive, allowing blessings to flow to me from many sources.

☙ Today, I admit my desires. I accept the path they suggest to me. If only one step at a time, I move in the direction of my dreams. I am alert, too, to my dreams moving toward me. I accept the forward motion of my heart's desire. I allow the Universe to answer my prayers and I am grateful for the support and abundance which I receive.

The boisterous sea
of liberty
is never without a wave.

<small>THOMAS JEFFERSON</small>

ℰ

L ife unfolds with sweeping vistas and hidden
valleys. Sometimes I see the shape of my future
shook out like a glorious silken cloth. At other
times, my future is concealed from me. I move forward
in faith but without the gift of vision. Such an alter-
nating reality of large strokes and small is normal to
most of us. Occasionally we know something very
large and are given the clarity and power to act on that
knowing. This is the woman I should marry . . . this is
the job I want . . . I should move west . . . this is my
new but important friend . . . Such knowings are piv-
otal and we know to value them. At other times, quiet

knowings come to us for smaller, more subtle adventures. I alter the path of my daily life and see a new face to my neighborhood. I rearrange the furniture in my house and discover more productive use of the space I have. These guidings, too, are the important stuff of life.

CA Today, I am led in large and small ways. I ask for vision and clarity and receive enough to steer my course. I accept my different forms of knowing. I cherish my seasons of clear-eyed vision and my times of simple faith.

Life rushes
from within . . .

WILLA CATHER

Cₑ

M y life is never barren, never without riches and gifts. In life's more difficult seasons, I remind myself that not all growth is seen. The Winter stores the promise of Spring within it. Even cold carries an ember of coming warmth locked in its icy heart.

Cₑ Today, I look past discouraging appearances. I focus on the wealth slowly germinating within me. I trust.

A friend
may well be reckoned
the masterpiece of Nature.

RALPH WALDO EMERSON

☙

Ours is a shared planet. Often, the spirit with which we give determines the spirit with which we receive. As we resolve to be gracious and hospitable, we notice a shift in others toward greater hospitality. The key to inhabiting a friendlier world is taking the time and care ourselves to make it a friendlier world. I take pen to paper and send a note to a far-flung friend. I pause to compliment a stranger on the beauty of his young dog. I comment to the waitress on the excellence of her service.

☙ Today, I act from my heart. I take the extra seconds to be warm and gracious with those I meet.

To be alive means to be productive,
to use one's powers not for any purpose
transcending man, but for oneself,
to make sense of one's existence,
to be human. As long as anyone believes
that his ideal and purpose is
outside himself, that it is above
the clouds, in the past or in the future,
he will go outside himself and seek
fulfillment where it cannot be found.
He will look for solutions and answers
at every point except the one
where they can be found—in himself.

ERICH FROMM

W hen our priorities are in order, our lives
flow with purpose and ease. Often the
very act of ordering and acknowledging
our priorities seems to cue the Universe to support us

in our goals. When our own house is in order, outer events appear to reinforce that ordering. What we know we need now appears.

C&. Today, I am clear in my goals and agendas. Today, I am focused and gently forceful in pursuing my aims. As I move ahead I am alert to options and opportunities which open before me. I am the arrow of desire flying true to its mark.

Give us grace and strength to forbear
and to persevere . . .
give us courage . . .
and the quiet mind . . .

ROBERT LOUIS STEVENSON

CA

Our griefs tempt us to isolation. Our sorrows lead us toward secrecy. The wounded heart is reluctant to show itself, fearful in its vulnerability of being wounded anew. The great mystery is that in connection lies our protection. In openness we find our shield. The soul is a field of wind-tossed grasses, touched alike by sun and snow. Sharing our trials lessens our burdens. Baring our secrets brings us solace and peace.

CA Today, I step forward out of isolation. I communicate to someone my heart's truth. I lay aside my defenses and allow my heart to be seen unshadowed by secrets or by sorrow. As I reveal myself, I am seen and accepted; I am protected and healed.

*Keep growing quietly
and seriously
throughout your whole development.*

RAINER MARIA RILKE

☙

A change for the good is still a change. Often we have held a shimmering dream that danced tantalizingly just beyond our reach. When, suddenly, that dream is ours, we may find we must work to enjoy it. We must consciously thaw our numbed emotions and allow ourselves the tingling sensation that our success is real. The moment we had so looked forward to is now at hand. Often our friends are as lost as we are. They, too, do not know how to behave. We must practice a forgiving heart toward ourselves and others as we blink uncertainly in the spotlight. We must seek out those who can love us before, during and after.

❧ Today, I pause to enjoy my success. I treat myself carefully knowing I am as much vulnerable as victorious.

If you can keep your head when all
about you
Are losing theirs and blaming it
on you . . .
Yours is the Earth and everything
that's in it.

RUDYARD KIPLING

D isappointment can darken our emotional
landscape like a gloomy day. Our spirits become downcast. A gray fog rolls in and the
landmarks that we look to for serenity and security become obscured. Depression clings to everything.
Nothing seems worthwhile. It is necessary to practice
a determined and practical optimism in the face of
disappointment. We must act rather than react, taking
small concrete steps to modify our mood. Sometimes
we need the challenge of a new major project. I will

sort my files, reorder my library, take a vigorous daily walk for a month. Sometimes it is as simple as buying fresh flowers or a pint of raspberries, or taking a refreshing bath. Sometimes it is placing a call to a lively yet sympathetic friend. Always there is a concrete way, however small, to act on our own behalf. The world may disappoint us but we can choose not to disappoint ourselves.

CB Today, I act with resilient optimism. I treat myself exactly as I wish to be treated. I am self-loving and self-respectful. I am the kind of person I myself respect and admire.

No duty is more urgent
than that of returning thanks.

SAINT AMBROSE

❧

Conscious living invites ritual, the sacred times and transactions we build into our daily life. A ritual may be as small as lighting a candle for our meals, listing our gratitudes at bedtime or even walking the dog. A ritual can be as humble as the weekly writing of postcards to our friends. Regular, repetitive and soothing rituals become the stepping stones through our days. They offer a gentle structure in times of flux. We endow rituals with meaning and rituals in turn bestow meaning in return.

❧ Today, I consciously consecrate a small action to the sense of the sacred in my life. Today, I honor my own unfolding by a prayerful attention to my own passage. I consciously link the sacred to the secular unifying my life.

Why stay we on the earth
except to grow?

ROBERT BROWNING

∽

The door to the future may stick when we try to open it. Not all transitions are easy or graceful. Sometimes our past is done before our future seems quite ready. We are caught in the corridor of in between, a limbo that feels awkward and uncomfortable. At times like these we must practice the art of containment. Soon enough the future will unfold, the door will swing open and the way be clear. In the meanwhile, we can consider the distance we have come already, the lessons we have learned and the chapters closed. By pausing to appreciate our growth, we find ourselves more restful than restless. The wheel will turn and find us ready.

Today, I pause to take stock. I count and appreciate my many gains. I rest before going forward. I savor the journey I've taken already and the distance I have come.

Learn to wish
that everything should come to pass
exactly as it does.

EPICTETUS

☙

Our emotional landscape is sometimes rocky. We feel deep chasms of loneliness, echoing canyons of despair. No matter how we cry out, our own voices come back to us. Our self-pity is amplified. We find ourselves drowning in the sea of our own heartache. "Where is God?" we wonder bitterly. "How could God allow this to happen to me?" Whatever the "this" is, it has also happened to others. There is no sorrow we are alone in suffering.

☙ Today, I embrace my humanity. I feel my emotions but do not allow them to isolate me. I reach out to others and myself with compassion and humility. I surrender to the river of life.

I do the very best I know how,
the very best I can.

ABRAHAM LINCOLN

◌

I am a pilgrim and I praise my progress. Finishing a large project brings us to a place of triumph and of grief. We have successfully accomplished our dream and now that dream, so long our companion, must give way to different dreams. There is excitement and loss in this eventuality. My dignity requires that I face both feelings, that I accept the "win" of a project brought to fruition and the loss of a long-cherished goal.

◌ Today, I celebrate my accomplishments even as I acknowledge my vulnerable feelings of closure. Today I salute myself as a work in progress, recognizing both the long road traveled and the road still ahead.

For good and evil,
man is a free creative spirit.

JOYCE CARY

❧

Sometimes a particular love is denied to us. The one we have chosen chooses someone else. We feel abandoned and betrayed. There is a seductive lure to bitterness. We are tempted to globalize our wound. "All" men or "all" women are the problem, the offenders, but this is not the case. I have simply been wounded and my wound, although painful, will heal.

❧ Today, I choose to cooperate with my healing. Rather than linger in self-pity, I reach out actively both for my own help and support and to offer those qualities to others. While I feel rejected by my beloved, I do not need to reject myself and I need not stifle my own capacity for love. Unable to love fully the one I choose, I choose instead to love fully those I can.

Two are better than one; because they
have a good reward for their labour.
For if they fall,
the one will lift up his fellow.
But woe to him that is alone
when he falleth;
for he hath not another to help him up.
Again if two lie together then
they have heat:
but how can one be warm alone?

ECCLESIASTES 4:9–11

We live life in community. The milestones celebrated by those we love also become our own as well. A child graduates and so, in a sense, do we. A spouse changes jobs and our job supporting our spouse shifts also. Strong and turbulent emotions may arise at another's rite of passage. We weep giving away the bride. A baptism or bar mitzvah fills us with pride and a sense of meaningful continuity.

෨ Today, I acknowledge and celebrate the important markers in the lives of those I love. I take the time and make the effort to communicate my joy at their passage. I open my heart to empathy and to sympathy, willingly sharing the joys and sorrows of those I love.

Move your sofa
and change your life!

KAREN KINGSTON

When we change our living space, we change our lives. When we take the time to order and nurture our environments, we bring to our own lives a sense of orderly flow. A chaotic, disordered habitat creates chaotic and disordered habits. Today I seek a spiritual alignment in my domestic space. I discard all that distracts me. I recycle what I no longer need. I do not allow guilt or sentiment to clutter my environment with things I do not love. I remember that "God" is the shorthand for "good, orderly direction."

Today, I put my life in order. I emphasize serenity and beauty in my surroundings. I allow increased cleanliness to prioritize my thinking. I create an environment that knows my highest goals and aspirations.

Man . . . is always an individual,
a unique entity,
different from everybody else.
He differs by his particular blending
of character,
temperament, talents, disposition,
just as he differs at his fingertips.
He can affirm his human potentialities
only by realizing his individuality.
The duty to be alive is the same as the
duty to become oneself,
to develop into the individual one
potentially is.

ERICH FROMM

W
e worry that we are not original. And yet,
the root word hidden in "original" is "origin." We are each the origin of our origi-
nality. We need not strive to be different from what we
are—rather, to be more fully what we are. Too often

we seek to change our very nature, asking it to conform to some stereotypical ideal. How much better to explore and accept our true nature, to see the rivers, canyons and plains of our temperament as beautiful and varied emotional geography.

 Today, I resolve not to change myself, but to accept myself. Today, I seek not to repress my nature but express it.

Our days flow like music. Allowing music to move through our days, we shape the symphony of life. Music teaches us the beauty of a carefully drawn solo trajectory. Music teaches us the grace of harmony. Music teaches us the importance of tempo and the need for rest. Music is a transcendent teacher and we can welcome the lessons that it bears.

Today, I open my heart to music. I take the time to appreciate and savor graceful notes. I allow music to teach and temper me. I conduct myself with musical aplomb.

In order that people
may be happy in their work,
these three things are needed:
They must be fit for it:
they must not do too much of it:
and they must have a sense of success
in it—not a doubtful sense,
such as needs some testimonial of others
for its confirmation,
but a sure sense, or rather knowledge,
that so much work has been done well,
and fruitfully done,
whatever the world may say
or think about it.

W. H. AUDEN

ork well done is its own reward. While praise for our labors is lovely, satisfaction comes from our own approval. In a work world that is harried and hurried, sometimes we alone notice our efforts and their effectiveness. The memo well written, the project brought to timely completion, the budget accurately spent, the team successfully managed—each of these can be a point of personal satisfaction.

⌀ Today, I am my own boss. I am my own mentor. I am my own critic, saying, "Job well done."

We never know how high we are
Till we are called to rise.

Ↄ

As they age, our parents become ours to protect and nurture as they once cared for us. As our roles reverse, as we find ourselves placed in the parental role of caretakers, many conflicting emotions may arise ranging from tenderness to anger and resentment. Despite our best intentions we may need to struggle for greater generosity than we in fact feel. A burden seeming too great to bear can yet be born one day at a time. We have within us stores of patience and practicality, intuition and invention, all of which are called to play during difficult times. Not one of is a saint, and yet we carry within our hearts the strength of ages. As we seek spiritual support and guidance, we find our actions tempered by humor and humility. The heart expands to love those we love as they need now to be loved.

∽ Today, I ask for the grace and courage to be strong and nurturing.

Whatever you think you can do
or believe you can do,
begin it.
Action has magic,
grace and power in it.

JOHANN WOLFGANG VON GOETHE

ew learning brings with it new wisdom. When we are willing to be beginners, the world is filled with adventure. Our intellectual life is a part of our overall health. By undertaking a course of study, we set in motion profound changes that illuminate our lives.

Today, I am willing to be a beginner. I am willing to start anew, to undertake humility in place of arrogance, to find my naïveté a loving companion.

True work requires true commitment. When we engage our hearts as well as our minds, our work life responds like a cherished lover. Too often we bring to our work a steely will that is without nurturing tenderness. Our work relationships bloom when we offer them devotion as well as discipline. A memo of praise instead of criticism, the moment taken to say thank you, the brief but public acknowledgment of another's contributions—each sheds nurturing light that encourages growth.

Today, I lift the lantern of my approval to light the path of my fellows. Today, I accept, acknowledge and affirm the contributions of others.

Despair is perfectly compatible
with a good dinner,
I promise you.

WILLIAM MAKEPEACE THACKERAY

When we are subdued and sad, our life is a brackish moor devoid of human habitation. In times of such despair, a concrete, civilizing action is often the most astringent antidote to the yawning inner abyss. A proper meal nicely served, freshly laundered sheets, a bedside bouquet, a cup of well-steeped tea, such small homely touches civilize the heart. A piece of beautiful music, the scent of fine furniture wax, a lovely candle burning on a sill—these small amenities draw us to our senses. Often we cannot answer the larger questions, yet we can cherish the small solutions.

☙ Today, I cherish my harrowed heart by concrete, loving actions. In the face of anguish I practice artful amenities. I allow my aesthetics to act as antidotes.

All my life I believed I knew something.
But then one strange day came when I
realized that I knew nothing.
Yes, I knew nothing.

EZRA POUND

Trauma can shake our certainty. The shattered faith of trust by a friend, the betrayal by a fickle lover, the cataclysmic loss of a long-standing job, the death of a young person—these and like events may skid us into despair. This is the rocky terrain of the heart, the moonscape of broken dreams. Every life contains times of spiritual bankruptcy, seasons of drought and doubt. Faced by a world made foreign of known markers, I set my own compass toward self-care. With prudence and wisdom, I schedule sleep, food, creation and recreation. Tending myself as I would an ailing friend, I gently rehabilitate my wounded heart.

༄ Today, I am a loving nurse to my ailing spirit. To-day, I salve my difficulties with personal compassion. I act toward myself with concrete loving kindness. I set firm but loving limits on my expenditures of energy.

Lukewarmness I account a sin,
As great in love as in religion.

ABRAHAM COWLEY

⬦

A waning of sexual potency may threaten our equilibrium. Accustomed to a certain standard of sexual performance, we may find ourselves threatened by shifts in libido. Yet a shift in sexual performance may trigger a rewarding shift in sexual practice. As invention replaces athleticism, ardor may replace rigor. It is the demand of the ego to be an athlete in bed. The heart seeks to encounter, not conquer, its lover. As I relinquish my need for sexual virtuosity, I open myself to new sensual experience. Allowing the art of connection to inform the act of love, I find ever-deeper levels of communication and satisfaction.

Today, I emphasize the love in my lovemaking. I express my passion in innovative and tender techniques. I allow my age and experience to season my sexuality.

Money is a singular thing.
It ranks with love as man's greatest
source of joy
and with death as his greatest source
of anxiety.

JOHN KENNETH GALBRAITH

꿍

A shift in our bank balance shifts our balance as a whole. The sudden windfall, the abrupt financial blow, either of these may send us spinning. Money is energy and a shift in its flow creates the need for an adjustment in our attitudes. A sudden spending spree leaves us hung over in its wake. A financial loss, whether catastrophic or chronic, leaches us of our capacity to feel personal power.

꿍 Today, I practice fiscal responsibility by facing fiscal realities. I aim for moderation and modulation of my fiscal flow. My worth is more than monetary.

*Above all, though,
children are linked to adults
by the simple fact
that they are in the process
of turning into them.*

Philip Larkin

Children mark our mortality. The landmark in our child's life is a landmark in our own. The toddler goes to day care and suddenly our days are free. The teenager leaves for college and our nest is abruptly empty. Our daughter bears a child, we bear the joy and the anxiety of her pregnancy. As our children grow more adult, we may face a childish impulse to keep them small. We are intended to guide our children, and yet their varying needs guide us through our own maturation.

❧ Today, I am kind to both the adult within my child and the child within my adult.

Talk of mysteries!
Think of our life in nature—daily
to be shown matter,
to come in contact with it—rocks, trees,
wind on our cheeks! the solid *earth!*
the actual *world! the common sense!*
Contact! Contact!
Who are we? *Where* are we?

LIN YUTANG

The one change we cannot change is change itself. No moment, however perfect, can be
maintained. Life moves on and moves us with
it. We are all works in progress, all developing parts of
a perfect plan. Only as we surrender to change can we
find permanence and peace. Only by being open to the
fierce flow of life can we find the steadying current.
The one thing that remains the same is that nothing

remains the same. As we accept and acknowledge life's passing nature, we are freed to cherish the moments that pass in bittersweet glory. No matter how difficult, life is beautiful. No matter how beautiful, life is difficult. This is the great paradox that opens the heart and brings compassion. We are all travelers on the vast and shifting sands of time. We are all inconsequential and important, very small and very large. Our transitions are like octaves building brilliantly upon each other. We are life's music, so let us dance.

୯ Today, I sing the song of change. I celebrate each moment as it passes. Today, I am a syllable of time and my voice is heard.

INDEX

Abundance   3, 37, 43, 113, 152, 164, 188

Adversity   26, 35, 100, 156

Ambiguity   28

Clarity   1, 48, 128, 144, 148, 150, 173

Compassion   97, 130, 166, 184

Continuity   139, 146

Courage   16, 89, 124

Curiosity   6

Expansion   4, 8, 77, 78, 131, 136, 141, 154, 171, 180

Guidance   12, 20, 39, 50, 54, 59, 71, 115, 126

Happiness   95

Health   73

Identity   45

Love   22, 31, 87, 107, 158, 168, 186

Music   175

Optimism   41, 56, 67, 79, 81, 102, 160, 182

Protection   93, 120

Relationship   10, 14, 24, 29, 52, 63, 69, 85, 111, 118,
      134, 138, 169, 181, 189

Satisfaction   176

Service   153, 178

Strength   46, 57, 83, 106, 167

Time   91, 117, 143

Unity   18, 61, 65, 75, 98, 104, 109, 122, 133, 162, 191

Work   33